OLD AMERICA

Villages

Lynn Stone

Rourke Publications, Inc.
Vero Beach, FL 32964

Edited by Sandra A. Robinson

PHOTO CREDITS
© Old Sturbridge Village: title page; © James P. Rowan: cover, 5, 9, 18, 20, 22, 23, 25, 28; © R. S. Arnold, Old Sturbridge Village: 13, 15, 16, 27; courtesy Old World Wisconsin: 29; courtesy Fortress of Louisbourg National Historic Park: 4, 7, 8, 11; courtesy Indian City–U.S.A.: 19.

Library of Congress Cataloging-in-Publication Data
Stone, Lynn M.
    Villages / by Lynn Stone.
    p. cm. — (Old America)
    Summary: Describes life in early American villages, including colonial and Native American settlements, and examines various living history or recreated villages.
    ISBN 0-86625-448-X
    l. Villages – United States – Guidebooks – Juvenile literature. 2. Villages – Canada – Guidebooks – Juvenile literature. 3. United States – Social life and customs – Juvenile literature. 4. Canada – Social life and customs – Juvenile literature. 5. United States – Guidebooks – Juvenile literature. 6. Canada – Guidebooks – Juvenile literature. [1. Villages. 2. United States – Social life and customs – Colonial period, ca. 1600-1775.] I. Title. II. Series: Stone, Lynn M. Old America.
E159.S78 1993
973'.09734—dc20   93-16152
                                   CIP
                                   AC

Printed in the USA

TABLE OF CONTENTS

I VILLAGES

Living history villages and museums have the look and feel of long ago.

It would be fun to leap back through time. What a great way to learn about the past! Too bad there are no machines to transport people back into the early days of America. The next best thing to time machine trips just might be visits to special village **re-creations**. These villages re-create the look and feel of villages from long ago. The best re-creations are living history villages and museums. Like many museums, they preserve human-made objects — **artifacts** — from the past. *Living* history villages also bring the past *to life*. There, people called character **interpreters** dress in the clothing of early North America. They demonstrate how the village stores, mills, farms and craft shops were

This re-created log cabin is located in New Salem State Park in Illinois.

operated two or three centuries ago. Interpreters answer visitors' questions about village life. Some interpreters have been trained to speak with the accents and phrases that were used by the early settlers of the village.

The **authentic**, or real, old-time look of a living history village comes in part from its buildings. Some buildings in the village may be new buildings that are made to look like buildings of the past. Others may be **restored**, or repaired, to keep their original appearance. These are the buildings that are originals — actual buildings that carpenters and bricklayers constructed many years ago.

Living history villages preserve a glimpse of what life was like in the small settlements of early North America. Through these villages, people can begin to understand and appreciate the ways of their ancestors. Long ago, most North Americans lived in villages. As many villages grew and became the cities of today, village life became only a memory.

The first permanent settlers from Europe arrived in North America after its "discovery" by Christopher Columbus in 1492. The first permanent European settlement on the American mainland was built by Spanish settlers at St. Augustine, Florida, in 1565. In the 1600s, British and French settlements sprouted in eastern North America.

A character interpreter carries dried codfish in the 18th century French town of Louisbourg.

People in early villages developed a sense of togetherness.

Early villages were little communities of homes, farms, churches and various shops. Most of the newcomers to North America had lived in villages or towns in their home countries. Living in a village again in the New World made them comfortable. Villagers were neighbors. They developed a sense of togetherness. They enjoyed each other's company, and they helped each other. They banded together to protect each other from enemies. As a village grew, it became a handy place to find goods and services without having to travel long distances.

II A COLONIAL AMERICAN VILLAGE

Plimoth Plantation re-creates an early 17th century colonial village in Massachusetts.

The early settlers in the Northeast were known as **colonists**. They founded settlements, or colonies, that were ruled by the settlers' native country, the country from which they had come. Britain, for example, considered North American settlements started by British settlers to be subject to Britain's rule. American colonial villages, then, were formed before there were American states. Massachusetts, for example, was a British colony before it was a state. The Colonial period ended in 1776, when the colonies declared themselves independent of Britain. After fighting against British soldiers for five years, the colonies won their independence and became the United States.

A typical Colonial village grew up near a stream or river. Fresh water was important for drinking and washing. It was also the source of power for **mills**. Mills ground vegetable grains into flour, and cut logs into boards. In addition, rivers provided a means of transportation by boat.

A typical village was made up of numerous homes, shops, a school, a meeting house, a church and a number of nearby farms. Each village usually had a sawmill, a gristmill, a tavern, a general store and an **apothecary**. The apothecary was the colonial version of our pharmacy or drug store.

The village had shops where wooden barrels, wagons, harnesses, wheels and guns were made. In those

Dressed in the clothing of the mid-1700s, a village baker is hard at work in Louisbourg.

days, more than two centuries ago, trees were plentiful. Many goods were made of wood. The blacksmith, however, was a metalworker. He crafted horseshoes, nails, wheel rims and fireplace tools.

The mills were great savers of time and energy. Both the sawmill and gristmill used the force of moving water to do their jobs. Water was dammed to create a mill pond, and then channelled through an opening called a spillway. The water rushed through the spillway onto a waterwheel. The water's force turned the wheel. The wheel, in turn, caused the grinding stone attached to it to do its work. This replaced the manual labor of people, or the work of horses or oxen.

III LIFE IN THE VILLAGE

Early American settlers often worked with their hands and backs. This is a picture of Old Sturbridge Village in Massachusetts.

Water powered the mills, but most labor in the old villages was performed by horses and oxen — or by people. Life was often difficult and uncomfortable. When Jamestown, Virginia, was established by British settlers in 1607, electricity was still nearly 300 years in the future. Water came from wells, not from faucets. Heat came from the logs burning in a fireplace, not from an oil or gas furnace. Evening light came from candle flames. Television, washers, dryers, vacuum cleaners, refrigerators and the rest of our electronic marvels did not exist.

People often died young. Many never reached adulthood — or even their second birthday. Doctors knew little about what caused disease or what cured it. A common treatment for illness was bloodletting. By cutting a patient and removing "bad" blood, doctors thought they could cure disease. We now know that these doctors were creating new problems — loss of blood and the risk of infection. Since there were no anesthetics, or painkillers, to make people unconscious during operations, patients often suffered terribly.

Early travelers moved on horseback, in horse-drawn carriages or by boat. Village taverns offered travelers meals, conversation and a bed for the night. For a few extra coins, the traveler could have a bed with sheets. There were no indoor bathrooms, and showers were unknown. Travelers washed up in log troughs outdoors.

A spinning wheel is used to make yarn before an open fireplace in a re-creation of early 19th century America in Old Sturbridge Village.

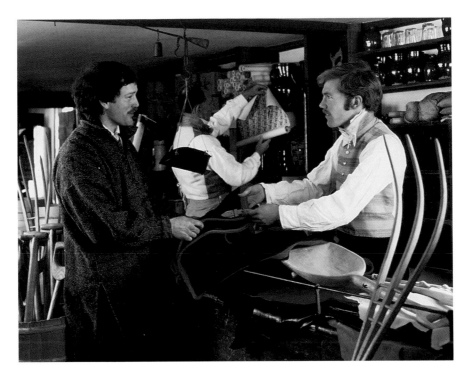

Villagers, like those in Old Sturbridge Village, shopped in general stores for a variety of goods.

Villagers shopped at the general store, the department store of its time. It carried just about everything settlers needed. In the early Colonial days, villagers "bought" goods by trading something for them. A farmer, for example, might trade meat or eggs for the planks and nails he needed. That kind of trade was called **barter**. Later, trade was conducted as it is today, through the exchange of money for goods and services.

Colonial children attended school in a one-room building. Regardless of age or grade, everyone shared the room. The teacher taught reading, writing and arithmetic to this mixture of children. Paper was scarce so students wrote on tablets of slate.

As difficult as the times were, life was easier in the village than out of it. Villagers knew that they could count on each other through good times and bad. At gatherings called "bees," neighbors gathered to help each other do such things as pick apples, husk corn, sew quilts and build new barns.

NATIVE AMERICAN VILLAGES

Mesa Verde National Park preserves the ruins of ancient Anasazi villages.

Native Americans lived in villages long before Europeans knew that North America existed. In what is now southern Colorado, Arizona and New Mexico, Native Americans built homes of bricklike adobe and rock. California's Pomo Indians built huts of weeds. Northwestern tribes fashioned wooden huts. Elsewhere, Native Americans built homes of earth, bark, grass and other natural materials.

Native American villages were generally not as permanent as the villages of the colonists. The villages that Southwestern Native Americans carved into rock cliffs were exceptions. Many deserted villages still remain.

Visitors inspect the dwellings of several Plains tribes at Indian City — U.S.A. in Oklahoma.

In Delaware, Ontario, Ska-Nah-Doht re-creates an Iroquoian settlement of 1,000 years ago.

One of the finest examples is in Mesa Verde National Park, Colorado, where the Anasazi (ah nah SAH zee) lived for 700 years, until about 1300.

The cliff dwellings of the Anasazi are ghost towns, but several Native American living history museums have been created. Saint Marie Among the Hurons re-creates a French settlement in a Huron village in Midland, Ontario. Ska-Nah-Doht is a re-creation of an Iroquoian settlement from 1,000 years ago. The Iroquois were a large tribe that lived in the Northeastern part of the United States and in parts of Canada. Chucalissa re-creates a 15th century Mississippian Native American village in Memphis, Tennessee. Indian City —

U.S.A., in Anadarko, Oklahoma, features the dwellings of several different Plains tribes. Many other re-created Native American villages scattered throughout North America also help visitors learn about the first American villages.

BUILDING A LIVING HISTORY VILLAGE

Character interpreters portray the militia, a local defense guard, in Colonial Williamsburg.

Virginia's former capital building stands in Colonial Williamsburg, a town that played an important role in American history.

With a bit of imagination, a visitor can sense the past in a living history village. The past is in the smell of sawdust and leather. It can be heard in the clang of the blacksmith's hammer. The sight of interpreters is a feast for the eyes. Creating a village that makes people *feel* the past is much more difficult.

Living history museums take their role as history teachers seriously. A great effort is made to be sure that every detail is just right. Consider Colonial Williamsburg, Virginia. It is of the finest outdoor living history museums anywhere. On the 173-acre site of this 18th century village, nearly 150 buildings have been restored or rebuilt. These projects have cost millions of dollars. To make sure its projects are as historically accurate as possible, Colonial Williamsburg hires dozens of researchers. They study old buildings and building plans, the ground where buildings once stood, and the human history of 18th century Williamsburg.

Historical research is important to all authentic living history museums. Researchers study old diaries, letters, books, public records, photos and drawings. Village re-creations are based on the information they find. After careful research, buildings can be constructed to match those from the past. Interpreters can be hired to accurately discuss with visitors what life was like in 17th and 18th century America. They can act out events that actually happened hundreds of years ago, like a wedding or trial. The things the interpreters say and do are based on hours of research, not on guesswork.

The Governor's Palace, one of nearly 150 original and re-created buildings in Colonial Williamsburg.

You may live near a living history village. They are scattered throughout much of Canada and the United States. A sampling of some of the best follows:

Colonial Williamsburg in Williamsburg, Virginia, re-creates the world of 18th century Virginia. Colonial Williamsburg is a remarkable place during all seasons. Character interpreters work at the same jobs and participate in the same day-to-day activities as the original settlers of Williamsburg. They create a real feeling of 18th century life.

Columbia State Historical Park in Columbia, California, is one of the best-preserved towns in the famous California gold country. Costumed guides and craftspeople help show what life in the village was like during the gold rush era of the mid-1800s.

Lincoln's New Salem State Park in New Salem, Illinois, re-creates the village where Abraham Lincoln lived from 1831-37. Also in the Midwest, 19th century Wisconsin lives again at Old World Wisconsin. Reconstructed buildings on 576 acres in Kettle Moraine State Forest show how several different groups of European settlers lived.

Old Sturbridge Village in Sturbridge, Massachusetts, authentically re-creates life in a rural New England village of the early 1800s. The village bustles with the activity of trades, crafts and farming. The working farms feature cows and other farm animals that were

A farmer feeds his long-horned cattle on a snowy day in Old Sturbridge Village, Massachusetts.

used by farmers in the 18th and 19th centuries. Some of these breeds are now rare.

Plimoth Plantation's Pilgrim Village in Plymouth, Massachusetts, is modeled after the Plimoth village of 1627, established by British colonists. The Plantation shows the different ways that the British and the local tribe, the Wampanoags, lived. Skilled interpreters speak in the dialects of British settlers. The *Mayflower II*, a full-sized reproduction of the sailing ship that brought the first Massachusetts colonists to America, is anchored nearby.

Among several living history museums in Canada is Acadian Village in North River, New Brunswick, a re-created village of the 1800s. The village recalls a time when French Acadians were returning to their homes after having been expelled by the British in 1755. The village has 40 buildings on a 3,000-acre site.

Black Creek Pioneer Village in Toronto, Ontario, re-creates rural life in early 19th century Ontario. Next to the village is the old Daniel Strong Farm and the original Strong house built in 1832.

The Fortress of Louisbourg National Historic Park on Cape Breton Island, Nova Scotia, preserves an 18th century community behind the mighty walls of old

At Plimoth Plantation, a Wampanoag demonstrates a lost art — crafting a dugout canoe.

It's haying time the old-fashioned way at Old World Wisconsin.

Louisbourg. Interpreters and careful reconstruction have brought part of the busy Louisbourg of 1744 back to life.

No, there are no time machines. Still, there are villages, like Louisbourg and Colonial Williamsburg and others, where time seems to stand still and the past is still present.

GLOSSARY

apothecary (uh PAHTH uh karee) - a drug store or pharmacy

artifact (ART uh fakt) - an object or tool made by people

authentic (awe THEHN tihk) - faithful to the original idea

barter (BAR ter) - to trade one thing for another; an exchange of goods or services

colonist (KAHL un ihst) - a person who settles in a country other than the one in which he was born, such as a colonist from England settling in the colony of Massachusetts

interpreter (in TER pret er) - one who acts out or explains an event

mills (MILLZ) - buildings with machinery for grinding grain or sawing logs

re-creation (ree kree A shun) - something that has been created to be identical to an original thing, such as a re-created building

restored (re STORD) - renewed, returned to the original condition

INDEX

31